White
Spells

Shine Your Magical Light into the World

You will love these simple, positive spells that brighten up your world and draw the good things in life to you. With candles, colors, special baths, crystals, and herbs, you can attract love and well-being while removing negative influences.

It's so easy, too! For instance, do you like baths? Try this.

Passionate evening spell

One by one, place the petals of three red roses into a bath with three drops of basil essential oil to enhance a night of passion and love. When you are in the bath, visualize a flame burning bigger than the universe itself. When you get out, gently pat yourself dry, collect the petals, and dry them with a white tissue, pressing them down hard. Put the petals in a little red bag with a teaspoon of dry saffron and place it under your pillow.

About the Author

Originally from Cuba, Ileana Abrev now lives in Sydney, Australia, where she is the manager of three well-known retail outlets. She has built a reputation for herself as a respected white witch among her customers and clients. With knowledge passed down to her from her father, an esteemed Santero, Ileana guides customers on a daily basis to solve problems with simple magic spells and positive visualization. Ileana has been a practicing witch for ten years.

Magic for Love, Money,
& Happiness

White Spells

Ileana
Abrev

2001
Llewellyn Publications
St. Paul, Minnesota 55164-0383, U.S.A.

First Edition
Second Printing, 2001

Book design and editing by Joanna Willis
Cover design by Lisa Novak
Cover and interior illustrations © Sandy Haight
Special thanks to Melissa Mierva for the herb precautions

Previously published as *White Spells: Wise women's secrets for greater love, health and abundance* (Moon Goddess, Sydney, Australia) © 1998 by Ileana Abrev.

Library of Congress Cataloging-in-Publication Data
Abrev, Ileana, 1959–
    White spells: magic for love, money & happiness / Ileana Abrev.—1st ed.
        p.   cm.
    Includes index.
    ISBN 0-7387-0081-9
    1. Magic. I. Title.

    BF1611 .A27 2001
    133.4'4—dc21

                                                                2001038055

Note: These spells are not to be used in lieu of professional advice.

Llewellyn Publications
A Division of Llewellyn Worldwide, Ltd.
P.O. Box 64383, Dept. 0-7387-0081-9
St. Paul, MN 55164-0383, U.S.A.
www.llewellyn.com

Printed in the United States of America

To Write to the Author

If you wish to contact the author or would like more information about this book, please write to the author in care of Llewellyn Worldwide and we will forward your request. Both the author and publisher appreciate hearing from you and learning of your enjoyment of this book and how it has helped you. Llewellyn Worldwide cannot guarantee that every letter written to the author can be answered, but all will be forwarded. Please write to:

Ileana Abrev
℅ Llewellyn Worldwide
P.O. Box 64383, Dept. 0-7387-0081-9
St. Paul, MN 55164-0383, U.S.A.

Please enclose a self-addressed stamped envelope for reply, or $1.00 to cover costs. If outside U.S.A., enclose international postal reply coupon.

To Beverly,
the most beautiful person in my life.

Contents

Chapter 3
Bath Magic . 29

Chapter 4
Herb and Plant Magic . 45

Chapter 5
Candle Magic . 63

spell / To send healing energies to a sick friend or family member / End an addiction spell / Protection from evil spell / For an enemy to be gone / Calm the home environment spell / To seek help from your guide / For stress / To help your child on the day of an exam

Introduction

$\mathcal{M}$agic has been a part of my life for as long as I can remember. I was born in Cuba and grew up with an intimate understanding of *Santería,* a magical practice that originated in Africa. Today in Cuba it is known as *Lucumí.* The people who practice Lucumí are known as *Santeros,* and are competent herbal and spiritual advisers. My father is a Santero, and thanks to his teachings I am aware of a world that holds secrets and mysteries at every turn.

Over the years I have used magic during desperate times and always had positive results.

What is magic? It is difficult to define magic. Contrary to popular belief, it is not supernatural. Magic is the use of natural energies and positive visualization to create change in our lives.

Each of us is magical simply because we are surrounded by energy. With this energy we have the power to bring good into our lives, or we can use it to attract negativity. The latter is destructive magic, and I want to make it clear from the outset that we should never wish unto others anything we would not wish unto ourselves. The Earth is full of living, vibrating natural wonders, and by utilizing its energies we can create magic. Why not do it the positive way?

Magic can be used in daily life to help with the visualization of our needs. A positive thought can be projected into the universe and become a beautiful aid for psychological transformation. Take prayer, for example. Prayer is a popular form of magic. It is energy sent out to the universe in a positive manner, and over time it is reflected back. Many dreams and desires have been fulfilled through prayer.

When performing magic we never have the right to take something that is not ours for the taking. For example, to break up an existing relationship for personal gain is destructive. If you want to perform this type of magic, know that you will have to live with the thought that this person never really loved you because you manipulated the love. Magic performed in this way never brings lasting happiness.

What is a spell? A spell is the use of natural products to help us manifest our immediate needs. So what is a white spell? A white spell helps us manifest our needs in a positive, unselfish manner and with a clean conscience. Above all, a white spell never harms or manipulates others to do our will out of jealousy, spite, or anger.

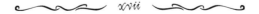

When carrying out your spell, take time to always listen to your heart and your conscience. Find out what your real needs are, and never let anyone make you do anything you are not ready for. The idea is to visualize your needs. Play them out in front of your mind's eye. If you want change in your life, desire it with all your heart. This is the power that drives your magic. This is the secret to manifesting your future.

At times we may have sought help from psychics and mediums for spiritual growth and allowed them to perform spells for us. Yet no matter how good or reputable they are, they do not have the same driving need as you to grow and evolve. You are the one with the actual problem and you see and understand your needs better than anyone else. So instead of paying someone else to perform a spell for you, do it yourself. You will be putting your heart and soul into it like no one else can.

Protection Prayer

The following prayer can be used before doing a spell for protection against negativity.

Oh, brightness, light of justice,
guide and protect me.
I have and hold divine love.
I shall strengthen the hand of justice
and weaken the hand of evil.
For the good of all, I wish it so.

chapter 1

Colorful
Magic

$\mathcal{E}$ach individual color in the spectrum gives out different vibration frequencies to our body and our everyday surroundings. Warm colors such as red and orange give out strong vibrations, while cool colors, like blues and pinks, give out passive vibrations.

We are light beings filled with colors known as the *aura*. Our aura changes according to the vibrations we give out. If you are stressed, you give out color signals associated with that stress to those around you. They know you are stressed not because you look scattered, tired, or are constantly having a bad-hair day, but they can feel the color signals you are

giving out. If you haven't noticed by now, stress can be catchy. It is because unconsciously we absorb those color frequencies that are a big part of how we relate to one another.

A good example of this is when you are the last one to arrive for a meeting. The room is filled with people and immediately you feel uncomfortable; all eyes are on you. When you entered the room, the room was already filled with color energies blending and mixing together. Then here you come from having some type of an altercation with the person that took your parking spot. Due to this inner anger your aura has gone from a pleasant yellow to a bright red in a matter of a millisecond. And you ask yourself why 90 percent of the people in the room are looking at you. It's not because you think you still have the tag showing from the skirt you purchased for the meeting, but because of the color frequency you are giving out.

We know color is a part of our life. Then why not use color to aid us in our everyday living? When you are stressed, the last thing you need is a red dress to really enhance the stress levels. Maybe pick something with cool colors like light blues or pinks to keep the stress factor on a lower frequency. Now if you are depressed, the last thing you need are cool colors or black. This is when you need a bit of those warm colors like reds and oranges to strengthen the emotions and to lift the cloud hanging above you.

We all experiment with color from time to time in the way we dress, the way we decorate our home, the color car we have, or even the clothes we dress our children in. You will see a change in your children's learning skills if they were to wear yellow, which is a learning color, and green, which is a growth color. The potential would be endless for them. Now if you chose to dress them in bright colors like red or neon red, you are asking for a day filled with mischief. It's like a sugar high to a child.

Healing illness with color works much in the same way. If you have a chronic condition you need to cool it, not heat it. If you wish to heal an ongoing illness, blue is the color to use. It gives out cool healing energies that are also protective.

Color in magic has its advantages and should be used at all times when conducting spells. Candle-burning rituals, such as the ones in chapter 5, are a very good way to use color when directing an intent to the universe to manifest. It reaches the universe by the way we portray our needs and wants.

The universal color for money is green, so naturally you will use green for your prosperity and money needs. Love has been associated with pink, like a young, innocent woman's blush when she speaks to the man she likes. Her aura turns into a bright healthy pink as it's filled with love and hope to

have her love returned in the same way. In the following chapters you will be using color to enhance your needs and wants to the fullest.

Below is a list of colors and their meanings. Use this guide to help enhance the power of any of the spells in this book. Add color to your wardrobe to enhance your needs and wants. Carry a colored cotton cloth with you at all times to manifest the dreams you wish to come true or to change your aura's frequency.

Amber	Develops psychic skills
	Enhances your sexual drive
	For communicating with spirits
	For a deeper meditative state
Black	Wards off negativity
	Removes hexes
	Protects against evil workings
	For truth in magical workings

Blue	Brings tranquillity to the soul
	Banishes anger
	Heals the body and the self
	For focus and relaxation before meditation
	Protects against others
Gold	Strengthens the mind
	For intuition
	For communicating with angels on the higher realm
	For money spells
Green	Brings luck in business endeavors
	Attracts money
	Aids spiritual growth
	Heals the emotions
	Good for children

Indigo	Useful when working with karma
	For meditation
	For psychic workings
Lavender	For spiritual development
	Works against stress in the home and at work
	Calms growing cancer cells
	Helps bring peaceful sleep
Orange	Promotes encouragement
Pink	Attracts friendships
	Brings love into your life
	To honor the self
	For communication between the self and spirit
	For self-love
Red	Enhances power
	For strength to fight against the odds

For sexual passion and a passion for life
Enhances sexuality
Relieves depression

White   Purifies the soul
For working with spiritual guides
Protects against dark workings
Brings justice

Yellow   Promotes learning in the young and old
Sparks intuition
Brings understanding when working
    with karma
For happiness in life

chapter 2

Crystal Magic

You work in harmony with the laws of nature when you work with magic, and crystals can be used as powerful magical tools. Crystals are minerals found all over the world. Ancient civilizations used them for healing and the art of magic. They also offered them to their deities to receive spiritual insight and guidance.

Crystals hold universal and Earth-bound energies that interact with an individual's energy to perform their magic. Each stone will feel different to each of us. For some people crystals feel warm; to others, cool. Some may feel a strong tingly sensation run up their arm when they hold a crystal, or perhaps a little lightheaded. Nearly all of us will find some type of inner peace when we hold one. We feel calm and relaxed because we have just made a bond with universal energies.

I believe crystals pick us. We can stand in front of hundreds of crystals of all different colors, shapes, and sizes and we will notice the one crystal that calls out, "Take me home!" It's as though this crystal knows your wants and needs, and with it you can manifest your deepest desires.

Crystals can be bought from New Age stores or any lapidary club or outlet. When you purchase a crystal, you must cleanse it when you get it home. Hundreds of people may have handled it, imbuing it with their own energies. It's important for you to cleanse it for your own well-being. There is no right or wrong way to cleanse a crystal. A small ritual I do to cleanse my crystals follows.

Crystal-cleansing spell

On a full moon night, take your crystal out into the yard and gently place it on top of the grass. Look up and see the moon shine on your crystal. Visualize a silver light from above penetrate your crystal's heart and see little silver flashes of light now inside the crystal on the grass.

Rub both hands together and pick up the crystal. Hold it in your hands and visualize the needs you wish the crystal will help and aid you with. Carry it with you at all times and do not let anyone touch it as it belongs to you and the moonlight.

In the following crystal spells I assume the crystals have already been cleansed unless noted otherwise. Where I specify using other materials such as lavender water or salt to cleanse your crystals, you can use the above ritual as a guide or make up a cleansing ritual of your own.

Spells are like rites of passage. They help you to focus on your needs and desires so they can in turn be manifested. The most vital ingredients for your spells are emotion, feeling, and love. If you are true to yourself and others, magic will never do you wrong.

Crystal Spells

For a growing puppy

Around the neck of your new best friend hang an amethyst heart to keep him or her from wrecking the house and backyard. (Note: Take care not to hang anything around a puppy's neck that he or she could get loose and chew or get caught on and choke.)

To help you reach your goals

Fill a bowl with rainwater and add a hematite crystal to it. Leave it in a place where it will not be disturbed for three days and three nights. On the fourth day, hold the crystal in your hand and visualize the goals you are reaching out for in life. See them manifest in your mind's eye, then simply wait until they do.

Money magic

In a clear, attractive bowl empty two cups of sesame seeds. Deep within the seeds hide a citrine crystal and a red jasper crystal. Place the bowl on your dining room table, and every month on the same date replace with fresh sesame seeds, keeping the crystal covered. Sit back and watch your money tree grow little by little.

When dealing with a legal matter spell

Place a bloodstone crystal in a bowl, add the petals of seven marigold flowers, then fill it to the top with water. Hold the bowl up high and say, *"Oh, petals of the sun, give this crystal strength to fight."* On the day of your legal hearing, take the crystal out and either hold it in your hand or put it in a pocket close to your heart.

Fertility magic

Place a small pumpkin under your bed. Cleanse a carnelian pendant necklace by placing it out in the sun for an entire day. Place the necklace on top of the pumpkin every night before you go to bed. Then every morning hang it around your neck and pick up the pumpkin and rub it around your navel and pelvic area. As you do this, visualize your desire to be a mother and see yourself breast-feeding your wanted baby.

This ritual should be done every day for three months. At the end of that time, take the pumpkin to a garden filled with flowers and leave it there. Wear your necklace at every hour, including during sleep.

When you've lost a loved one spell

Bring an amethyst crystal close to your heart. It will remind you of the love, joy, and laughter you shared with your loved one. The crystal will help to heal the loss.

To attract love

On a piece of parchment paper write the characteristics of the person you wish to attract (do not use a name). Cleanse a rose quartz crystal with three drops of rose oil. Wrap the piece of parchment paper around the crystal and tie a pink ribbon around it. Bury the bundle under a rose bush on a Thursday at the stroke of midnight and say, *"Oh, Mother Earth, I give thee the person I wish to attract. May only beauty and goodness be seen in me by the person you hold deep within."*

Dig up your crystal on Friday at the stroke of midnight and leave a seed of a flower behind. Carry the crystal and its bundle with you at all times, especially when you are near the person you wish to attract.

To enhance sexual drive

Place carnelian in a white bowl with water. Add a teaspoon of salt and leave it outside for three days and three nights. When the time is up, hold the crystal close to your heart, visualize your desires and needs, and imagine making passionate love by the sea with the one you love so deeply. Keep the crystal in a red cloth bag and leave it under your pillow.

For a loved one not near

Cleanse a crystal geode that has been sliced in half in a bowl of salt water (water with one teaspoon of salt added) once during the day and again at night for three days. Keep one half and send the other to your loved one. No matter what the distance, you will always be together.

For a lover

Place a tiger's-eye crystal in enough fresh rose petals to cover the crystal and leave it in a very special place for three days. When the time is up, hold the crystal tight and visualize your love penetrating it like a lightning flash. Give the crystal to the one you love with this thought in mind.

Stay faithful to your lover spell

Take a lodestone crystal to a tree with a bird's nest in it. Rub the crystal on the tree and say, *"Faithful I shall be like the birds nesting in this tree."* Take the crystal to bed and place it under the sheets where the pillow lies.

Uncover your true feelings spell

In a bowl full of water add three drops of rose oil, the petals of a single rose, and a sodalite crystal. Leave for three days. After the third day, remove the crystal and keep it close to your heart. It will help you to uncover your true feelings.

Rid anger at self and others spell

Bury a blue lace agate crystal deep in the roots of a lavender bush. Leave it for seven days and dig it up on the eighth day after 3:00 P.M. Hold the crystal in your hand, bring it close to your heart, and say, *"Blue lace agate with your calming blue, open my heart and take my anger so I may not direct it at myself nor another."* Wrap the crystal in a blue cloth and always carry it with you.

Protection against an enemy spell

Place seven rusty nails and seven black peppercorns in a clear bowl. Fill it with water and add a pinch of salt. Place a clear quartz crystal, a tiger's-eye crystal, and an Apache tear crystal in the bowl. Mix everything together, visualize protection from the one that wishes you harm, and say, *"Stay away my enemy, do me wrong no more."* Let the bowl sit for twenty-four hours, then place the crystals in a little blue drawstring bag and carry them with you at all times.

Whisk away fear spell

Leave an aquamarine crystal in the sun for three hours. When it is warm, hold it in your hands and visualize heat entering your head. Think of nothing but the heat of the sun. The fear will subside and the crystal will give you strength to face each day.

Protection for the house spell

Leave four clear quartz crystal points outside your house on the night of a full moon. Pick them up the next day, hold them tight in your hands, and visualize protection for your home. Place the crystals inside your house, one at each of the four corners with the point facing toward the outside (i.e., toward the back or front yard). As you place each crystal say, *"With this crystal I protect my home from negative energies and bad entities."*

Stress-releasing spell

Place seven amethyst crystals in a tall glass of water. Cover with a paper towel and leave outside for the night. Before the day starts, strain everything through a fine sieve or cheesecloth and drink the water. You will feel calm and totally purified.

For study and exams

Obtain a citrine crystal and a fluorite crystal and place them in a white bowl. Fill the bowl with water and add a teaspoon of salt and three drops of rosemary oil. Leave it outside for three days and three nights. On the fourth day, hold the crystals in your hands and visualize excellent grades. Keep the crystals with you at all times when studying or taking exams.

To find employment

In a bowl of water drop a red jasper crystal, three cinnamon sticks, and a teaspoon of sugar. Leave this in a private place where the moon can shine on it for three nights and four days. Then hold the crystal in your hands and visualize the work you wish to find. Carry the crystal close to your heart at all times.

For dream recall

Cleanse a smoky quartz crystal in lavender water (water with two drops of lavender oil added) each night before you go to bed and then place it under your pillow. Keep a note pad and pen at arm's length. Write your dreams down as soon as you awake but before you get out of bed. As soon as your feet touch the floor, your dreams fade.

To combat insomnia

Place two drops of pure lavender oil on an amethyst cluster. Hold it in your hands just before slumber. Visualize peaceful thoughts and happy dreams. Place the amethyst cluster in a purple sock under your pillow and go to sleep.

Peace in the house spell

Place a rose quartz cluster in a large bowl and add water and three drops each of lavender and lemon oils. Let it sit for a day or so, then hold the bowl in your hands and visualize harmony and blissful peace. Place it in the room where arguments take place most often and you will soon experience harmony.

Make a wish spell

Select a crystal that you are attracted to. Cleanse it with the cleansing ritual at the beginning of this chapter or with one of your own. Hold it in your nonwriting hand. Visualize your deepest desire, then see that desire penetrate the crystal. Take the crystal to a running stream and throw it as far as you can into the stream. As the crystal travels, your wish will follow.

chapter 3

Bath
Magic

$\mathcal{A}$ bath connects us to the water element, and with the aid of herbs, crystals, and essential oils we can enhance its power. Having a bath nourishes the whole body, and the special properties of the herbs, crystals, and essential oils used can bring about a positive state of mind, as well as promote health and well-being.

Creating a magical bath with herbs, crystals, and essential oils can be further enhanced with positive visualization. This is when real magic is brought into the bathroom, encouraging relaxation and assisting in the manifestation of your dreams. When you get out of a bath enjoyed in this way, you will feel a lightness of being, as though you are walking on air. Your body will feel slightly tingly, and positive energy will be bouncing around you. The negative energy will spin down the drain when you let the water out.

The magical bath spells that follow use a lot of the old Santería ways and will inspire exploration and provoke laughter. In a magical bath it is important that you wet your hair. And the longer the bath, the better. No soaps or any kind of cosmetic detergents should be used. If you wish, have a full shower and wash your hair before you enjoy your magical bath.

After your bath but before the water is drained, collect everything you have put into the bath, and, if not specified in the spell, dispose of it anywhere except in the garbage bin. Finally, gently pat yourself dry after a magical bath to seal in the magic.

If you don't have a bathtub in your home, you may use the ingredients in a bucket filled with warm water. Then slowly let the water run from the top of your head to your toes.

Bath Spells

Prosperity spell

Draw a bath and to the water add a tablespoon of almond oil, half a cup of dried oats, ten seeds from a ripe tomato, and the petals from three tulips. Settle into the bath and visualize your wants and needs, imagining yourself manifesting them. After the bath, collect the tulips and oats, dry them in the sun, and then sprinkle them in front of a bank. Do this every Thursday for two months.

For money

In a saucepan bring five cups of water to a boil. Add a handful of fresh parsley, basil, and mint leaves. Drain the herbs and keep the water for the bath. As you mix the herb water with the bath water, imagine money coming to you, and after you are in the bath, think only of financial security.

To bring abundance

Add as much fresh basil, parsley, and alfalfa to a warm bath as you'd like. Also place the petals from a red flower in the bath for determination. Visualize abundance, see it happening in your mind's eye. When you least expect it, it will come.

To enhance psychic ability

Add a bunch of fresh celery, one teaspoon each of dry saffron and thyme, five large bay leaves, a small bunch of honeysuckle, and two large cinnamon sticks to a bath. Visualize a rainbow of colors emerging from your third eye and getting larger and larger and connecting with the universe.

To attract love

Put three large cinnamon sticks, a bunch of fresh basil, seven cooking cloves, and six cups of water into a large pot. Place the pot on the stove and bring to a boil. Drain the herbs and empty the water into your bath. Add the petals of a pink flower, a daisy, and three pansies. (Note: Choose your flower carefully to avoid allergic reactions, harmful effects from oils, etc.) Sink in and feel the loving energy all around you. Imagine your aura changing to a loving, passionate red. Repeat this spell for three consecutive days, beginning on a Friday, the love day.

For luck

Add to your bath a cup of pineapple juice to sweeten any sour thoughts. Visualize everything working out just as planned.

To attract women

Add five bay leaves and one teaspoon of crushed fresh ginger to your bath. Visualize as many women as you can, and imagine yourself embracing them. Do this on Tuesday because this is when Mars attracts. After the bath, collect the leaves and dry them in the sun. Carry them with you in a little red drawstring bag at all times.

To attract men

Draw a bath and add one teaspoon of barley and the petals of three pink flowers. (Note: Choose your flowers carefully to avoid allergic reactions, harmful effects from oils, etc.) Sit in the bath and visualize the man you want in your life. Do this on Friday when Venus attracts.

Before going out on a date spell

Draw a warm bath while holding three red roses close to your heart. Petal by petal, drop the roses into the bath with thoughts of a possible new love. Add a teaspoon of dry damiana, gently sprinkling it in just before you bathe. In the bath, visualize your date and how you would like it to end.

Passionate evening spell

One by one, place the petals of three red roses into a bath with three drops of basil essential oil to enhance a night of passion and love. When you are in the bath, visualize a flame burning bigger than the universe itself. When you get out, gently pat yourself dry, collect the petals, and dry them with a white tissue, pressing them down hard. Put the petals in a little red bag with a teaspoon of dry saffron and place it under your pillow.

Find your soulmate spell

Peel three apples. Add the peels to the bath together with one teaspoon each of dry barley and lemongrass to spice things up. Sit in the bath and visualize your soulmate. Do this for seven days, beginning on a Friday. After each bath gather the peels of the apples, dry them (but not in the sun), and keep them behind your front door.

Before a bride's wedding day spell

In a bath add six drops of lavender essential oil and seven different colored flowers. (Note: Choose your flowers carefully to avoid allergic reactions, harmful effects from oils, etc.) Gently recline in the bath and relax.

For colds and flu

Collect a bunch of fresh eucalyptus leaves, break them in half with your hands, and place them into the bath with five drops of eucalyptus oil. While in the bath, imagine a clear, fresh forest and its pure refreshing scent.

After an illness spell

Draw a bath and in it add the petals from three white roses, three white gardenias, and three white carnations, with a sprinkle of dry rosemary. Do this on Sunday, the healing day.

Cheer the soul spell

Slice an orange and a lemon in half and place them into a bath with three drops of neroli essential oil. Like the steam in the bathroom, imagine any heaviness of the heart slowly dissipating.

Purify the soul spell

Draw a bath and to the water add the milk of one fresh coconut and the petals of a white flower. (Note: Choose your flower carefully to avoid allergic reactions, harmful effects from oils, etc.) Visualize yourself rising to the heavens, feeling free and full of love, with universal energies dancing all around you. You are connected and purified.

To break negativity

Place half a cup of vinegar, a bunch of fresh rue, and a tablespoon of salt in your bath. (Note: Rue can cause dermatitis upon contact with skin.) Light a white and a blue candle close to the bathtub. Imagine yourself as pure light, with nothing entering you but pure universal energy. Visualize the negativity leaving every pore of your body.

Anger-dispelling spell

Draw a bath and add five violets and their leaves and three drops of lavender essential oil. When you sit in the bath, remember that a word said in anger hurts not only yourself but others around you. It eats away at peaceful energy.

To stop gossip

Add a fistful of cooking cloves and two teaspoons of dry blessed thistle to your bath. Visualize a barrier going up between you and the gossip to keep it at bay.

To settle children for the night

Give your children a bath with a few drops of lavender essential oil added to it. They will magically drift off to sleep.

Dream at night spell

Add seven jasmine flowers, a bunch of holly, and three drops of peppermint essential oil to your bath. Visualize yourself dreaming and enjoying your dream world. Enjoy this bath directly before retiring.

Feel protected and secure spell

Gather as many three-leaf clovers as you can (of the kind with white flowers that have not been recently sprayed with pesticide or herbicide), either at home or at the local park, making sure the stems are attached. Place the clovers in the bath with three sticks of chopped celery. Visualize yourself as a knight wearing a shining armor that protects your body and soul. Know that no one can penetrate your shield.

Make a wish spell

Get two large sunflowers and drop them petal by petal into the bath with a fistful of crushed sage. (Note: Do not use sage if you are breast-feeding; it can dry up the mammaries.) Sink into the bath and visualize your wish up in the clouds, floating in the heavens and being nursed by loving hands. Imagine your wish materializing.

Herb and Plant Magic

erbs are one of the most important tools you can use for magic. For centuries, they have been used for their healing and magical properties. Today, our pharmaceutical medications are simply synthetic versions of what our ancestors used to use.

Like humans, plants connect to the four elements: air, water, earth, and fire. Without these elements, plants and humans could not possibly exist. We all need air to breathe, water to drink, earth to feed from, and fire for warmth and light. But at times we take our environment for granted. When was the last time you admired a wildflower in a field, or touched a mighty oak tree? This is something a lot of people don't get to do every day, and as a consequence they lose touch with nature. Remember, one of the most prominent colors in the world is green. It signifies growth, which brings understanding, courage, prosperity, and healing.

All herbs and plants grow above ground. From the smallest shrub to the tallest tree, they feed sacred spiritual energies from the womb of Mother Earth. Once dried they can be used for incense when burned on a charcoal tablet. The charcoal is placed in the middle of your censer and once lit it gives out a dark smoke. After the initial smoke disperses, the charcoal tablet becomes red hot. This is when you can add your magical incense.

Always remember, when picking leaves from a plant to do magic, cook, or when cutting flowers to give to a loved one, never pull it totally from its

roots. Always ask permission from Mother Earth when clipping and leave a token as a form of payment or thank-you, like a crystal or a new seed of any kind.

Herbs can also be used as *amulets*. Amulets are charms or ornaments used for protection or for an intent. They can be seen in jewelry or carried in little bags which I refer to in this chapter as "drawstring bags." You can purchase these bags if you wish, or you can make your own with a piece of cotton material of the color specified for the particular spell you are doing and simply place the contents in the middle, make a bundle, and tie it at the top with some string. Following is a number of herbal amulets you can make to use at home or work, or for protection against the negativity that may seep into your everyday life.

Herbal Amulets

Money magic

In a green bowl mix one teaspoon each of powdered ginger, Irish moss, and sesame seeds. Crush together to form a powder, and as you crush it visualize your money needs.

Light a charcoal tablet and on top add a quarter teaspoon of your money powder. Concentrate, breathing slowly and steadily. Do this for ten minutes every night for seven nights, beginning on a Thursday night just after the sun goes down.

For money in your purse or wallet

If you find yourself without a cent, sprinkle dry sassafras in your purse or wallet and you will always have enough for the things you need to buy.

Prosperity spell

Sprinkle fresh alfalfa sprouts in the front and back of your house. As you do this, visualize your most wanted needs and recite the following: *"May the ground take this offering I give. May it bring me prosperity which is in great need."* Do this seven times every Thursday, and don't be shy—sprinkle plenty of alfalfa sprouts.

Female fertility spell

Find a bunch of fresh mistletoe and leave it indoors to dry until it becomes brittle. (Note: Mistletoe berries are poisonous; do not ingest.) Place the dry mistletoe inside a little orange drawstring bag. Carry it with you everywhere you go, and at night place it under your pillow. It will strengthen the female reproductive system.

Male fertility spell

If you want to enhance your fertility, eat lots of carrots, carrot seeds, and bananas in groups of threes. It will aid performance like never before, with sperm count levels way up.

To find love

Dry three apricot seeds. Make yourself a little pink drawstring bag and drop the seeds inside with three drops of ylang-ylang essential oil. Visualize positive thoughts of love in your life.

Love note

Write a note to the one you love on a Friday evening, then gently rub a bunch of lavender buds on the notepaper. Blow the buds to the wind and say, *"May the fragrance of lavender carry my thoughts to the one I love."* When your love opens this note, nothing but your loving thoughts will matter.

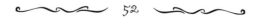

To attract women

In a little cup add three drops of sandalwood oil, two drops of cedarwood oil, and one bay leaf. Mix together and let stand one night under a full moon. As you set the cup on the grass say, *"Strength and magnetism this leaf shall have, no female will ever resist the male energy it has, attracted they will be to the male they see in me."* Carry the leaf every time you go out and you will attract lots of females.

To attract men

In a little red drawstring bag insert a teaspoon of dried catnip and hang it around your neck. Like a cat that goes crazy when it smells the "magical scent," so, too, will men be attracted to your scent.

To enhance sexual drive in men

In a little red drawstring bag insert three acorns, the top of a green banana, and three shells of oysters you had consumed and dried in the sun for three hours. Keep this close to your lower extremities (like in your pants pockets) and you will see a change for the better in your sex life.

To enhance sexual drive in women

Get one dry typha leaf (better known as cattail) and while visualizing your sexual needs, place it in a little red drawstring bag. (Note: It is illegal to gather cattail in some areas.) Keep it with you at all times.

To attract friends

Make yourself a little pink or purple drawstring bag. Let the peels of one lemon dry for three days. Then put the peels in your little bag and add a teaspoon of passionflower petals and a bloodstone crystal that has been cleansed with lavender essential oil. Hold this little bag in your hands and visualize yourself in a place full of people, talking, laughing, and having fun. Keep this little bag with you when you need a friend around.

Protection for the house spell

With a red ribbon, tie a bunch of garlic to the corner by your front door. It will protect you and your loved ones from negative vibes that may enter your house. Never let anyone use the garlic for anything else.

Protection against intruders spell

Get a fresh, whole coconut, drain it, and cut it in half. In a bowl mix one teaspoon each of fresh rosemary and basil and half a cup of uncooked rice. Blend these together, then fill both halves of the coconut with the mixture. Fit the coconut together and wrap a white ribbon around it to keep it shut. Go outside on a Sunday night and bury it in the backyard. It will protect your home and backyard.

To rid negative forces from the home

At the front and back doors of your house hang two bunches of clover upside down. As you hang each bunch, feel the negative energy around you and direct it to each bunch. The clover will then set out to fight the negativity around your house.

Protection from evil spell

Make four little blue drawstring bags, each the same size. Mix in a bowl two teaspoons each of dry angelica, Solomon's seal, and balm of Gilead buds. (Note: Fresh angelica closely resembles poisonous hemlock which can be fatal.) As you do this, visualize your house protected from evil. Divide the mix into four equal amounts and fill each bag with it. Hang or hide the bags in the four corners of your house.

Courage spell

Sprinkle a pinch each of dry yarrow and thyme in your shoes. (Note: Yarrow can cause dermatitis upon contact with skin.) While you wear them, your fears will stop and you will have the courage to accomplish what you have set out to do. It will encourage self-worth and make you feel ten feet tall.

Improve the mind spell

In a little yellow drawstring bag place three vanilla beans broken in half, a bunch of fresh rosemary, and the petals of a lily of the valley, and wear it around your neck. (Note: The leaves of lily of the valley can cause skin irritation.) With each breath visualize your mind becoming stronger, remembering dates you will not want to forget.

For a job interview

In a jar big enough to fit a hand's full of crushed pecans, add three drops of rose oil, and keep a lucky hand (root of an orchid) inside with the lid shut tight. After three nights, place your lucky hand and the crushed pecans in a little red drawstring bag, and take it with you to job interviews. With this little bag you will feel confident while questions are being asked, and you will have a good chance of getting the job you want. Don't let anyone else see the red drawstring bag.

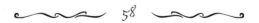

For those who play to win

In a green bowl mix together one teaspoon each of poppy seeds, dry angelica, and dry chamomile. (Note: Fresh angelica closely resembles poisonous hemlock which can be fatal.) As you do this, visualize winning not only at cards, but at everything you do. Put the herbs in a little green drawstring bag and carry it with you at all times.

For sleeping problems

Make yourself a little purple drawstring bag, and as you do this think of having a good night's sleep. Inside, add a teaspoon of dried valerian, and each night hold it in your hand while you lie in bed. Before you know it you will be soundly asleep, and when you awake, the little bag will be somewhere in your bed.

For spiritual awareness
and psychic strength

In a medium-sized jar half-filled with almond oil add a teaspoon of dry yerba santa, damiana, and spearmint leaves, with seven drops of lime essential oil. (Note: Spearmint oil is toxic and the leaves can cause dermatitis.) Mix together with a plastic spoon and screw the lid on top. This is to be used before spiritual healings or for divination purposes. Place three drops on your hands before you start, rub them gently together, and place on your forehead. Then bring your hands to the back of your neck, breathe deeply, and start your work. You may even like to use this blend in your bath.

For astral traveling

In a little purple drawstring bag place two teaspoons each of dry angelica and crushed peppermint leaves, and add a smoky quartz that has been cleansed with lavender essential oil. (Note: Fresh angelica closely resembles poisonous hemlock which can be fatal; also, peppermint oil is toxic and the leaves can cause dermatitis.) As you do this, visualize what you would like from the astral realm, and every night before you go to bed rub the drawstring bag on the bottom of your feet. This will take you where you want to go and protect you along the way.

Candle
Magic

Candles are more than just decorative lighting for dinner parties and romantic evenings. The flame of a candle emits universal energy. It also brings light into our lives, not only so we can see in the dark, but for our spirit to communicate with the heavens.

The flame of a candle can be likened to the human spirit. No matter what the circumstances, we all have a living flame within. This flame dwindles at times when we lose hope and our future seems dark and uncertain. But we can rekindle the flame over and over again, and it will burn until our work here is done.

Humans have often used fire to pay homage to higher powers. It's now time to pay homage to ourselves, for in reality *we* are the higher power. We are the ones who can bring creation or destruction into our lives.

Candle-burning unites our spirit with the candle's flame. With visualization and concentration, a candle can act as a beacon, sending messages to the universe. When you visualize your desires, try to do it in a positive manner, and respect the destinies of others—they are not yours to change or play with.

Candle-burning can become complicated because of the different colored candles used. I have made this type of ritual as simple as possible, but there are things you must know before you start.

When partaking in the rituals that follow, you may want to find a special place where you will not be disturbed. You will need a medium-sized card table covered with a white or purple cloth. This will be your altar. You will also need candle holders and an oil burner that you may purchase at any outlet that carries aromatherapy oils and essences.

Your altar will always have two candles on it for the day of the week. The altar candles will change color depending on the ritual being done. In each ritual, I will tell you which colors you need.

In many spells I have not specified how long a spell should last; that depends on you and your time. Just remember that the more concentration and visualization you put into any of the spells, the better the outcome of your intent.

Use the list below as a general day-by-day guide. You can also use the candles for times when you want to enhance the specific attributes that the color of the candle represents. For example, if you want to nurture strength and passion, burn a red candle. You can burn it on any day of the week; it doesn't necessarily have to be on its designated day.

Sunday	Yellow to aid healing of the self and for learning something new.
Monday	White for purity and protection.
Tuesday	Red for strength and passion.
Wednesday	Purple for wisdom and family communication.
Thursday	Blue for patience and tranquillity.
Friday	Green for love to grow in your life.
Saturday	Black to rid negativity from the week that has just passed, and to promote positivity for the week that is coming.

In a lot of the rituals you will need to use a candle of the color associated with a person's astrological sign, called an *astral candle*. For this, refer to the following list.

Aries	March 21–April 19 White
Taurus	April 20–May 20 Red
Gemini	May 21–June 21 Red
Cancer	June 22–July 21 Green
Leo	July 22–August 22 Red
Virgo	August 23–September 22 Black
Libra	September 23–October 22 Black
Scorpio	October 23–November 21 Brown

Sagittarius	November 22–December 21
	Gold
Capricorn	December 22–January 19
	Red
Aquarius	January 20–February 18
	Blue
Pisces	February 19–March 20
	White

Once you decide on a spell, purchase tapered, colored candles that burn the same color from beginning to end. The whole candle must be the color nominated, that is, don't use candles that are white inside.

The candle is divided into two parts. From the middle up toward the wick is called the *North Pole,* and from the middle down is known as the *South Pole.* Now that you know this, you can start to *dress* the candles before the ritual. To do this, search your kitchen for some olive oil, vegetable oil, wheat germ oil, almond oil, or coconut oil. Rub a small amount of oil in your hands, pick one candle up at a time, and with your right hand rub up toward the North Pole, and with your left hand rub down toward the South Pole. Never rub the candle in an up and down motion. As you do each candle, visualize your needs and wants and why you want to do the ritual.

Some of these spells may continue over a few days, but if it is not specified, you should finish the spell on the same day. There is no need to purchase more candles unless some of your candles burn quicker than others. If you do need to purchase another candle, dress it accordingly. Never blow a candle out for you will blow away the candle's energy. Instead, use a snuffer or your fingers.

Once you have finished your spell you may still have some candles left over. Never use these candles again for a new spell. You may use them around the house, but not for an intent. And whatever is left on your altar cloth, dust it to the wind.

Also, be aware of fire hazards. Never leave candles unattended or alone with children.

Candle-Burning Spells

Attain success spell

Light two blue altar candles on a Thursday night, and burn three drops of lime essential oil in your oil burner. In a small bowl place some crushed nutmeg, and sit back and visualize your intentions for success.

Next, light your astral candle and around it light four orange candles. Sit or stand, and in your mind's eye see the success you wish to have. Every five minutes bring the orange candles closer to the astral candle. After the candles are grouped, spread out your arms, look up at the heavens, and finish the ritual by saying, *"Flame of these candles, I reach out to the universe for strength to bring me success. I need it now. My intentions are to harm no one, and this is the only way I wish to gain it."* Let all the candles burn to the very end and repeat when success is needed.

For money

Light two blue altar candles on Thursday after dusk, and by the side of each place two bunches of fresh basil. Around each bunch of basil sprinkle poppy seeds, and imagine money walking through the front door in any shape or form.

Next, light your astral color candle in the middle of your altar table while still visualizing money. Then at each side of your astral candle light two green candles and say, *"Hear me, oh Divine, I'm calling thee. With these candles I send you my money needs. Find it here or there, I really don't care, but bring it to me so I may feed my money needs."* Do this for fifteen minutes, then snuff the candles. Repeat for five consecutive days, and as you do this every day move the green candles a bit closer to your astral candle so that at the end of the five days the three candles are as close as they can be and are working on your money needs.

Successful business spell

Light two blue altar candles on Thursday just before the full moon, visualizing your business and what it needs. Burn three drops of basil essential oil in your oil burner and light three frankincense tears (frankincense incense cones) on your censer to keep away negativity.

With your business still in mind, light five green candles if your business is open five days a week, six if open six days a week, and so on. Burn the candles every morning for thirty minutes for seven consecutive mornings, and watch your business grow. Repeat when things are slow or when you feel it needs another push.

Find the perfect mate spell

Light two green candles on a Friday night. On a char-coal tablet add a pinch of dragon's blood powder (*Daemonorops draco; Dracaena*) and a bit of crushed cinnamon stick. While you do this, visualize your perfect mate.

Next, light your astral candle in the middle of your altar. Light four pink candles around your astral candle, and make sure that you place one of each of the pink candles to face north, east, west, and south. In the middle, sprinkle petals from pink flowers, prefer-ably roses, then say, *"I call all the corners of the world: north, east, west, and south. Hear me: I am looking for my mate, and I need your help to find him/her. Search for me, high and low, and I will be waiting with open arms for this person to come into my life."* Sit back and watch the candles burn in unison while the universe searches for your perfect mate. Let the candles burn right to the end.

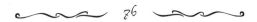

To be asked by your lover
for your hand in marriage

Light two red candles on a Tuesday night. Burn three drops of rose essential oil in your burner, and on top of your altar table scatter the petals from two red roses. While you are doing this, visualize the way in which you would like your lover to propose to you.

With this in mind, place your lover's astral candle in the middle of your altar and around it light three red and three pink candles alternatively in a circle. Say out loud, *"As these candles burn, so alight my desire to wed. [Name of lover] and I have been together for a long time. We have talked about marriage and now with this spell I hope to initiate a proposal. There is a mutual love and respect between us, so if it is to be, let love conquer all."* Sit back and relax while visualizing the wedding day you have always dreamed you would have. When you are ready, snuff the candles and repeat for three consecutive nights.

To heal a marriage

Light two purple altar candles on Wednesday and tie a red ribbon around something you both shared that once brought you together in love and laughter. Place this item in the middle of your altar, and burn two drops of patchouli essential oil in an oil burner.

Next, light an astral candle for each of you, then light a red and an orange candle and place them on each side of your partner's astral candle while visualizing strength and love. See your marriage as it is and what you would like it to be. See yourselves talking and coming to an understanding about what has gone wrong and how you can heal it. Then say, *"I don't know if I deserve the loneliness I feel. I am willing to work to heal whatever is missing. Our love still burns like the flames of these candles. Oh, Divine, make my love's heart glow with happiness once again. Make me understand his/her sadness. By Lady Venus, I wish it be.*" Relax and think of what you have just done. Snuff the candles. Do this ritual for three consecutive days, and always remember that communication is the key to a healthy marriage.

Meditation spell

Light two white altar candles on any day of the week. Burn three frankincense tears (frankincense incense cones) on a charcoal tablet, and for a little bit of inspiration add a pinch of crushed mandrake root on top. (Note: Mandrake root is poisonous; do not inhale.)

To open up your third eye, continue by lighting two purple candles. In the middle of them place a lapis lazuli crystal that has been cleansed with lavender essential oil. Start your meditation as usual, and repeat whenever you meditate.

To calm the anger of a loved one

Light two purple altar candles on a Wednesday in the name of the person you wish to calm down. Place a lotus root on your altar and visualize the tranquillity and peace you wish your loved one to have. (Note: It may be illegal to gather water lily [lotus] roots in some areas.) Burn three drops of lavender essential oil in your burner.

Next, light the person's astral candle, and with seven light-blue candles make a circle around it. As you burn the candles, bring this person to mind. See him or her being angry, then becoming less and less so until you can bring a smile to his or her face. Send out thoughts of peace and love, imagining tranquil seas or a mountain calm and strong. Snuff the candles. Do this ritual every Wednesday for as long as needed.

Find love within spell

Light two green altar candles on a Friday night, and as you do this visualize the love you wish to cultivate within—a love without reservations or hate. Bring to your altar a bunch of fresh pink flowers and have them displayed in a vase. Feel the freshness and beauty they bring. Smell them and feel the peace.

Next, light five pink candles in a circle, and in the middle place a rose quartz cluster that has been cleansed with salt water (water with one teaspoon of salt added). Under the cluster place a piece of paper with your name on it. Visualize the flames warming your heart and say, *"I am a good person, I love who I am. No longer will I feel anger or hate inside me, only gladness that comes from knowing and accepting who I am and what I will become."* Do this for about fifteen minutes, then snuff the candles. Repeat only on Friday for seven consecutive weeks.

For luck

Light two yellow altar candles on Sunday and burn three drops of vetiver essential oil in your oil burner. Sprinkle crushed nutmeg on your altar table and visualize bringing luck into your life.

Next, light a black candle and see all your bad luck being consumed with the flame. Then light two green candles for growth and hope, and see your luck changing. As you stand back, visualize your needs. Then lift your hands high and say, *"Let luck come into my life, and may it change it. I am a simple soul, searching and wondering if I am worthy of all my goals. I mean no harm to others, I just want to get on with my life and leave behind all my bad luck."* After ten minutes, extinguish the candles. Repeat every evening for three consecutive days.

Overcome an illness spell

Light two yellow altar candles on Sunday and sprinkle crushed eucalyptus leaves on your altar table.

As you visualize yourself being healthy and on top of the world, light an orange candle. On each side of the orange candle light a red candle, then stand back, and watch the flames burn your illness away. Sense the strength within you to overcome your illness and say, *"I will no longer thirst on weakness. My strength will help to heal me, and I will regain my health."* Snuff the candles and repeat every Sunday until a change in health can be seen by you and others.

To send healing energies
to a sick friend or family member

Light two yellow altar candles on Sunday. Crush a fistful each of dried calamus and peppermint leaves together until a powder is formed. On a charcoal tablet burn a quarter teaspoon of this powder while thinking of the person you would like to send well-wishes to. On a piece of parchment paper write down the person's name and on top of it light his or her astral candle.

While still focused on the illness of your loved one, light four white candles and two red ones, and in front of them light a black one. With the black candle visualize the person's illness melting away, with the white candles visualize him or her healing, and see the red one giving him or her strength. Snuff the candles, and if you wish, do this ritual every Sunday until you see the person getting well, then repeat once a month to help keep up his or her courage and strength.

 84

End an addiction spell

Light two red altar candles on a Tuesday night. In the middle of your altar place the addictive substance that you would like to give up (e.g., a cigarette, alcohol, or some type of drug). Cover your addictive substance with a black cloth and around it wrap a black ribbon. Visualize yourself despising it with an intensity only an addict can have.

With this in mind, light your astral candle and around it light seven red candles for courage and strength. Stand by your altar and bring to mind the pain, the hurt, the lies, and the abuse that an addiction can inflict. As the candles burn so will your desire for the addictive substance. Snuff the candles and repeat every day for seven consecutive days while you go cold turkey. You may do this ritual for a loved one too.

Protection from evil spell

Light two black altar candles on a Saturday night, and crush one teaspoon each of blessed thistle and rue into a powder. Light a charcoal tablet and add the powder, but only a little at a time. Add two or three frankincense tears too (frankincense incense cones). While all this burns on your charcoal tablet, think of the evil you wish to be gone.

With this in mind, light two white candles to represent the purity and truth of your heart, and two red candles to give you strength and courage to fight the evil. Then light a black candle and feel the evil fade as the candle melts. As this is happening say, *"I'm stronger than the evil around me. I'm pure and white with nothing to hide. May good overthrow evil at every turn."* Let the candles burn for half an hour, then snuff them. Repeat for two consecutive nights.

For an enemy to be gone

Light two black altar candles on Saturday, and as you do this visualize the wrongs your enemy has inflicted on you. Burn three drops of frankincense essential oil in your oil burner to clear negativity, and on a piece of parchment paper write the following: *"Be gone my enemy [name of enemy]. Be gone and never set foot on my front door."*

Immediately light a black candle and place the parchment paper under it. Then light a pink candle and say, *"[Name of enemy], find love instead of hate; find peace and love within your soul. Let me be, and stay away from me and my loved ones."* Sit back and visualize your enemy walking happily away, leaving you alone once and for all. Snuff the candles and repeat every day for seven consecutive days.

Calm the home environment spell

Light two purple altar candles on a Wednesday and burn three drops of lavender essential oil in your oil burner. While you are setting this up, meditate on the household concerns that are stressing you out.

Next, light a blue, pink, and orange candle, and as you do this visualize peace, tranquillity, and harmony being established between you and the people you are living with. Step back and watch the flames burn, then say, *"Disharmony be gone, bring peace to this home."* Meditate for ten minutes on the love and peace your home needs, then snuff the candles. Repeat every night for a week.

To seek help from your guide

Light two white altar candles on any day of the week. As you do this visualize your guide being around you and say, *"I need your guidance on this day."*

Once focused, place in the middle of the candles on the altar a vase full of fresh white flowers and say, *"These are for you for always being here for me."*

Fill a glass with water and place it on your altar table and say, *"This water is to bring you clarity and spiritual growth."*

Light two purple candles, then sit down and talk to your guide about what is troubling you. You will begin to feel a sense of peace that only your guide can bring, and before you know it you will have your answer. Visualize for as long as you wish, and repeat the ritual whenever you need advice or guidance from your spiritual guide again.

For stress

Light two white candles on any day of the week. Burn one drop of ylang-ylang and two drops of lavender essential oils together in your oil burner. Feel the peace around you as you relax and unwind for a few seconds.

Next, light two blue candles for peace and tranquillity, and between them place an amethyst cluster. Feel the energy of this crystal calm you.

Then, while still focusing on the peace and tranquillity that you greatly need, light an orange candle and see its color surround you and free the stress. Once finished, sit down, relax, and visualize all the stress leaving your body, going back to where it came. Let the candles burn right to the end. You may do this ritual as often as needed.

To help your child on the day of an exam
Light two yellow altar candles and burn three drops of rosemary essential oil in your oil burner. Visualize your child sitting down with the exam papers, ready to begin.

With only thoughts of your child in mind, light an orange candle to give him or her courage and concentration to go through with the exam. Then light a blue candle and visualize your child relaxed. Last, light two yellow candles to enhance his or her intellect. Stand back and look at all the candle flames for a few minutes. Visualize your child reading and writing without hesitation as the questions are answered carefully and knowingly. Let the candles burn until your child gets home, then snuff the candles. If you wish, conduct this ritual every time a test comes your child's way.

Afterword

These spells are for individual growth and evolution. We don't want to infringe on others, assume we know what others desire, or want anyone else to be other than who they are. The spells work best when we wish for change in ourselves. We can then become healthier, happier, and more abundant, radiating a light that will in turn attract what we want in life. Remember, we already hold the greatest power to our own evolution; when we visualize what we want, it does appear.

Glossary

Altar

A sacred place created for magical workings.

Altar candles

Two candles placed on an altar to represent the day of the week.

Amulet

A charm or ornament used for protection or for an intent.

Astral candle

A candle of the color associated with an individual's astrological sign.

Astral realm

A parallel universe that is not physical but a mirror image of ourselves and the things around us.

Astral travel

Separation from the self; an out-of-body experience where you are aware of what is around you.

Aura

Invisible colors that radiate outside a physical form.

Censer

A small container used for burning incense.

Charcoal tablet

A special kind of charcoal that when lit can be used to burn dried herbs.

Cleansing crystals
Purifying crystals using natural energies. For example, salt and water prepare crystals for individual needs.

Dressing candles
A ritual conducted to ready candles for an intent.

Guide
A spiritual guide or guardian angel.

Herb
A plant—annual, biennial, or perennial—that dies back each year. There are aromatic, culinary, and medicinal herbs.

Karma
The law of the universe that keeps the balance of right and wrong.

Lucumí
An African-based religion now being practiced in Puerto Rico and Cuba. Better known as *Santería*.

Magic

    The use of natural energies and positive visualization to create change in our lives.

Magical baths

    Baths that are taken with natural energies to manifest dreams, to relieve stress, and to establish a connection with the water element.

Mind's eye

    Used to see visualizations in one's mind as if they were movie clips.

Mother Earth

    The spirit of the planet Earth.

North Pole

    A name given to the top of a candle, from the center to the wick.

Oil burner

    A deep ceramic dish with a tea candle on the bottom used for burning essential oil.

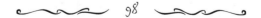

Parchment paper

Originally, a paper that was made out of animal skin. Today, imitations may be purchased from office supply outlets.

Ritual

The act of preparing the spiritual self by gathering magical tools and conducting magical workings or any type of religious act.

Santería

A magical practice that originated in Africa.

Santero

A competent herbalist and spiritual adviser in the Lucumí tradition.

Snuffer

A tool used to extinguish candles.

South Pole

A name given to the bottom of a candle, from the center down.

Spell

A combination of focusing on your needs while using positive thought patterns and some of nature's natural energies.

Third eye

Known as the sixth chakra, located in the middle of the brow. The third eye is the center of our creative perception which works with our subconscious mind to enhance psychic abilities.

Visualization

The art of concentration used for seeing and making things happen.

White spell

Any spell conducted for a positive outcome that does not use the manipulation of others.

Spell
Worksheets

$\mathcal{Y}$ou can create your own spell book (also known as a Book of Shadows) by purchasing a blank notebook and writing out the same questions from the following pages.

Spell Worksheet

Date spell conducted:

Reason for conducting the spell:

The way you were feeling before the spell:

The way you were feeling after the spell:

Time it took for the spell to manifest:

Noticeable changes made by the spell:

Spell Worksheet

Date spell conducted:

Reason for conducting the spell:

The way you were feeling before the spell:

The way you were feeling after the spell:

Time it took for the spell to manifest:

Noticeable changes made by the spell:

Spell Worksheet

Date spell conducted:

Reason for conducting the spell:

The way you were feeling before the spell:

The way you were feeling after the spell:

Time it took for the spell to manifest:

Noticeable changes made by the spell:

Spell Worksheet

Date spell conducted:

Reason for conducting the spell:

The way you were feeling before the spell:

The way you were feeling after the spell:

Time it took for the spell to manifest:

Noticeable changes made by the spell:

Spell Worksheet

Date spell conducted:

Reason for conducting the spell:

The way you were feeling before the spell:

The way you were feeling after the spell:

Time it took for the spell to manifest:

Noticeable changes made by the spell:

Index

☾ REACH FOR THE MOON

Llewellyn publishes hundreds of books on your favorite subjects!
To get these exciting books, including those on the following pages, check your local
bookstore or order them directly from Llewellyn.

Order by Phone
- Call toll-free within the U.S. and Canada, 1-800-THE MOON
- In Minnesota, call (651) 291-1970
- We accept VISA, MasterCard, and American Express

Order by Mail
- Send the full price of your order (MN residents add 7% sales tax)
  in U.S. funds, plus postage & handling to:
  Llewellyn Worldwide
  P.O. Box 64383, Dept. 0-7387-0081-9
  St. Paul, MN 55164–0383, U.S.A.

Postage & Handling
- **Standard** (U.S., Mexico, & Canada). If your order is:
  $20.00 or under, add $5.00; $20.01–$100.00, add $6.00
  Over $100, shipping is free

(Continental U.S. orders ship UPS. AK, HI, PR, & P.O. Boxes ship USPS 1st class. Mex. & Can. ship PMB.)

- **Second Day Air** (Continental U.S. only): $10.00 for one book +
  $1.00 per each additional book
- **Express** (AK, HI, & PR only) [Not available for P.O. Box delivery.
  For street address delivery only.]: $15.00 for one book + $1.00 per
  each additional book
- **International Surface Mail:** Add $1.00 per item
- **International Airmail:** Books—Add the retail price of each item;
  Non-book items—Add $5.00 per item

Please allow 4–6 weeks for delivery on all orders.
Postage and handling rates subject to change.

Discounts
We offer a 20% discount to group leaders or agents. You must order a minimum of 5 copies of the same book to get our special quantity price.

Visit our website at www.llewellyn.com for more information.

Silver's Spells
for Protection
Silver RavenWolf

What do you do when you discover that your best friend at work sabotaged your promotion? Or if a neighbor suddenly decides that you don't belong in his town? *Silver's Spells for Protection* contains tips for dealing with these situations, and more.

This book covers how to handle stalkers, abusers, and other nasties with practical information as well as magickal techniques. It also covers some of the smaller irritants in life—like protecting yourself from your mother-in-law's caustic tongue and how to avoid that guy who's out to take your job from you.

1-56718-729-3
264 pp., 5³⁄₁₆ x 6, illus. $7.95

Spanish edition:
Hechizos para la protección

1-56718-731-5 $9.95

To order, call 1-800-THE MOON
prices subject to change

Silver's Spells for Love

Silver RavenWolf

Does your current relationship need a spicy boost? Have you been browsing for love in all the wrong places? Maybe you want to conceive a magickal baby? From finding a new lover to handling that couch potato partner, *Silver's Spells for Love* has more than 100 ideas, potions, and incantations to bring titillating passion into your waiting arms. Whether you want affection, commitment, or a hot time on the town tonight, this book will teach you the nuances of spellcasting for love!

1-56718-552-5
312 pp., 5⅜₆ x 6, illus. $7.95

Spanish edition soon available:
Hechizos para el amor

0-7387-0064-9 $9.95

To order, call 1-800-THE MOON
prices subject to change

Silver's Spells for Prosperity

Silver RavenWolf

Take charge of your finances the Silver way! Now one of the most famous Witches in the world today shows you how to get the upper hand on your cash flow with techniques personally designed and tested by the author herself. She will show you how to banish those awful old debts without heartache, get money back from someone who owes you, and transform your money energy so it flows in the the right direction—toward you! An abundance of spells can aid you in everything from winning a court case to getting creditors off your back.

1-56718-726-9
240 pp., 5⅜ x 6, illus.   **$7.95**

Spanish edition:
Hechizos para la prosperidad

1-56718-730-7   **$9.95**

To order, call 1-800-THE MOON
prices subject to change

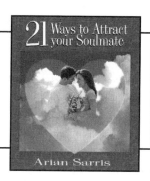

21 Ways to Attract Your Soulmate

Arian Sarris

You can't easily bring in your soulmate just by wishing. You need to light up like a Christmas tree, so the right one can't miss you! How you do that is the purpose of this book. First you will learn what a soulmate is, and the two kinds of soulmates. You will discover how to clear out the old to let in the new, and how to summon the help of your Higher Self and your angels. The book contains 21 exercises designed to help you dream your soulmate into reality, change the magnetic attraction of your aura, cut the cords of old relationships, create a soulmate talisman, and much more.

1-56718-611-4
264 pp., 5⅜ x 6   **$9.95**

Spanish edition soon available:
Compañeros del alma

1-56718-613-0   **$9.95**

To order, call 1-800-THE MOON
prices subject to change

Coin Divination
Pocket Fortuneteller

Raymond Buckland

If you've ever flipped a coin to help you make a decision, you've already practiced the art of divination, or fortunetelling. Now, for the first time, a book is available that shows you how to expand on the art of coin divination so you can examine your present and future anytime, anywhere.

From the simplest single coin toss to the more complicated *I Ching* and tarot readings, you will learn how to answer any question or shed light on any dilemma, whether it involves career, love, family, money, or health.

1-56718-089-2
240 pp., 5¾6 x 6, illus.   **$9.95**

Spanish edition soon available:
El lenguaje de las monedas

1-56718-104-X   **$9.95**

To order, call 1-800-THE MOON
prices subject to change

Candles, Meditation, and Healing

Charlene Whitaker

Now you can read and influence your own future through the magic of candles. It's easy! Candles are an extension of your consciousness—symbolic of persons, places, and things. When you ask that they represent something or someone in your life, they become very powerful. Light the candles and tap into a source of "enlightenment" and guidance on choices pertaining to career, romance, health, children, and personal growth. Do readings for yourself and friends, send healing energy to those in need, and amplify the power of your prayers and meditations. This book shows you how.

1-56718-818-4
176 pp., 5⅜₆ x 6   **$7.95**

Spanish edition:
Las velas

1-56718-822-2   **$9.95**

To order, call 1-800-THE MOON
prices subject to change

Celebrating the Crone
Rituals & Stories

Ruth Gardner

Throughout history, the passage into Cronehood has been ritualized. In many cultures, the Crone was welcomed as the revered elder of the circle. Ritual is the oldest and most successful method of experiencing truth in a deeply meaningful way.

Celebrating the Crone is for those women who want to experience the power of a personal aging ritual. You will find guidelines for conducting your own Croning ceremony, and you will see the many different ways that other modern women have chosen to honor the spirit of the wise one within.

Embrace the silver hairs, the wrinkles, the change of life. Grab your friends, bring a copy of this book, and celebrate your rite of passage from Maiden to Mother to glorious Crone.

1-56718-292-5
240 pp., 5⅜ x 6, illus.   **$12.95**

To order, call 1-800-THE MOON
prices subject to change